ALTERED

LANDSCAPES

A PICTORAL GUIDE TO MADNESS

By

CHRISTINA MILLER

ARTIST

Christina Miller

DEDICATION

Dedicated to all those in despair, in the dark halls of depression and the calliope of madness.

Also, thank you Dr. Jeffrey Collins for all your effort on my behalf.

CONTENTS

Christina Miller

AUTHOR'S NOTE

I wrote this little tome in 1990, or thereabouts, as I don't really recall the exact date. All the images included in this book are from the time when I was in and out of mental hospital stays for the five years between 1988-1993. All the language and descriptions are also from this time, excepting slight changes.

I remember sending off my hand painted sample book to a publisher, who it was I can't remember now; but some weeks went by and a woman called me from the publisher and told me that while they did not publish art books, she was so very moved by my work and just wanted to let me know. It was this woman, and her very kind thoughts, that led me to remember over the years, that I had ever compiled it at all.

A special thanks to my daughter Ana for all her patience and love throughout the years.

MAD TO MADDER

There I was, three days later, watching with a quiet horror the asphalt groan, crackle and split, shooting jagged black fissure all around the tiny structure I was working in. My heart paused. I tried to breathe, knowing that these cracks were surely only in my mind, and that the evil spirit beneath the ground who was pushing up the road, was only a figment of my imagination. This thought soothed my troubled mind and the fissures disappeared. I had escaped my own hallucinogenic gargoyles. I rested. Then as I drew in deep gulps of ocean air something stirred in the trees. Not a bird or small animal, something large. It also groaned. Not human. The woods around me grew quiet, and abysmally dark. I could hear other beings. The woods began to crackle. The things moved in closer. My will, my mind could not dispel the nightmare this time. More than fear, I felt hunted. I picked up the radio speaker and called the dispatcher, asking if a ranger could come and relieve me, as I was not feeling well, not at all.

I thought I would get over being strangled; it wasn't as though I was dismembered or dead or raped. Everyone else at the work seemed quite matter-of-fact about the whole thing.

A trip would get me away, I could relax, quit this job, and I would see friends. Get over it! I was a mom, I had been

Christina Miller

through a lot already in life, and this was just a matter of getting some…peace?

A therapist I had sought out because the ground under my feet opened up leaving me standing on a glass road beneath which was with a huge hellish mouth, jaws gaping open about to eat me, had suggested after taking me to a psychiatrist that I needed to go into a hospital. No way! A trip was all I needed. Get away, take a rest, and relax!

Six weeks later I was in a whole new town, and a psychiatrist did put me in a psychiatric hospital after I had called him up concerned about the panther that was stalking around my room, it was the blue one I had been painting earlier that day, and also told him there were ten or so creatures from other dimensions crowding my bed, and said, "I thought I would be all right as long as they didn't touch me."

This book of my paintings chronicles a journey to an unknown world. Wherein visual reality merged with my subconscious and produced the altered landscapes you are about to see. The journey did not take just a few weeks, or months but rather years to return to reality.

"Depressed"

My will, psyche was obliterated, death before the body dies, my heart a nuclear meltdown, the prison of this pain whipping its barbwire around me. My brains blowing away like 100 bullets ripping off the top of my head. My body and self was disappearing.

Christina Miller

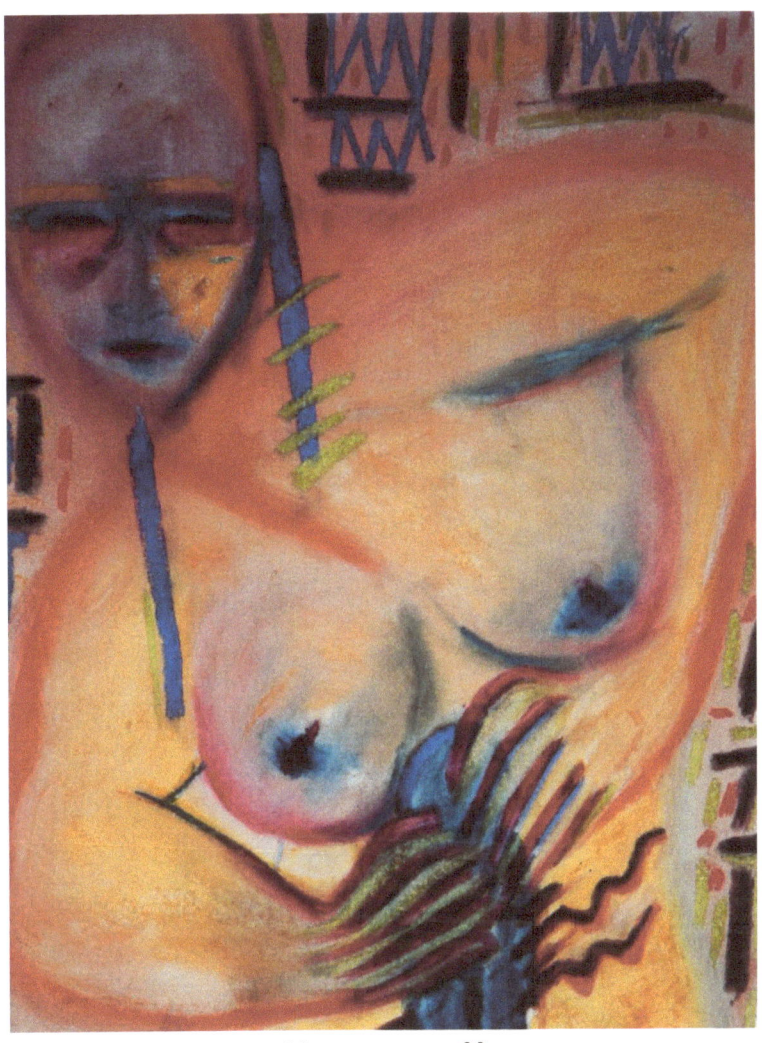

"Torn Out"

An alien language surrounds me in cryptic forms, decipherable only to my unconscious; this blue thing, abortion, being , is torn out of my belly. I am sightless. Riding in a car, this yellow creature came out of me like so much ectoplasm. I felt a wrenching as it escaped my body.

Christina Miller

"Two Selves"

Two selves, two personalities at war with one another, the blue hating the other, the other insane and stupid, in pain, ineffectual. The path leads to a chair of lightning bolts of destruction; an electric chair. I feel a violence towards self that leads to death.

Christina Miller

"Down"

Down. Real down. Suffocated by anger, confusion, and suicide. My selves are mere emblems, hidden in chaos. My mind is broken and despairing.

Christina Miller

"Masks"

The room I am stuck in, the open door for some future time when I can stop fooling myself. I refuse to be angry; I refuse to allow the fear to be real. My mask of sensibility wags its tongue. I am ill, sick unto death of myself. No center, no self, endless.

Christina Miller

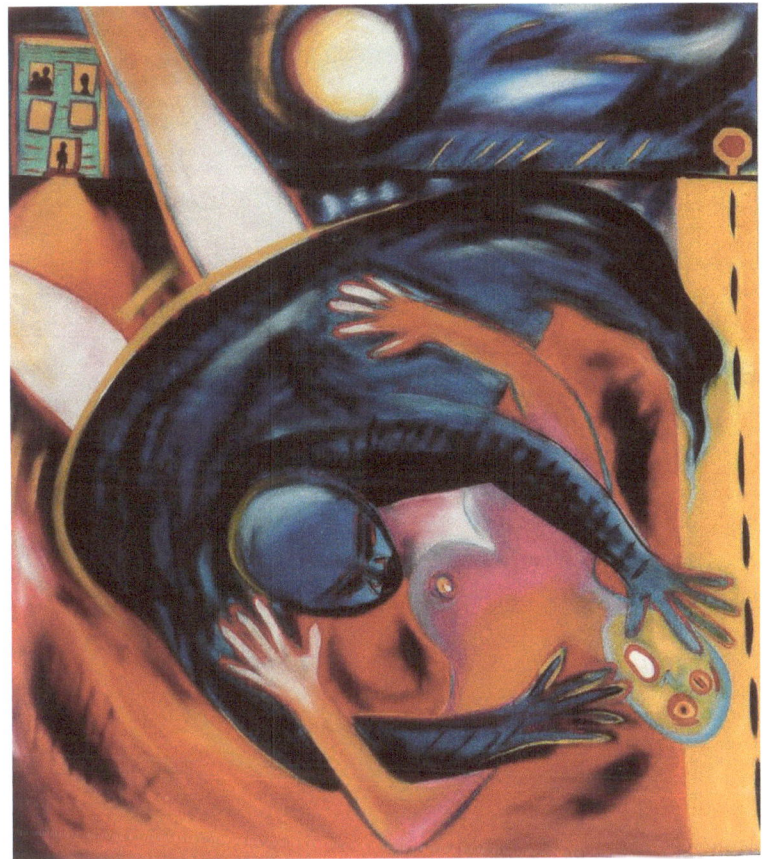

"Terror"

Terror of attack, how familiar it feels; it is on a road to nowhere. Others look on in curiosity, fear, knowing. They stay in their rooms. It has taken me two years of therapy to be able to paint this. (Two years after being strangled in the park.)

Christina Miller

"Terror of the Unknown Self"

After seeing so many selves, this one is unfamiliar. It is a ball rolling slowly toward me, I am a cartoon, hysterical character, it is coming toward me with a great moaning and creaking. This painting scared me the most.

Christina Miller

"I Enter Hell"

The disk in my hand contains the voices that lead me further into darkness. I no longer recognize myself. The landscape is alien and at war.

Christina Miller

"I Eat Myself"

I eat myself; eaten in an Hellish orgy of anger and catatonic despair. It reminds me of my childhood.

Christina Miller

"Wolf and Moon"

I divide into two selves. Moon is soft, destroyed, and bludgeoned, an altered body full of scars. Wolf moves, I can feel it escape at night to run off into the wild desert.

Christina Miller

"The Sun King"

The Wolf divides, becomes My soul, Myself. Now in forms of panting dogs with great red scars across their hearts. My analyst stands near, but off the path, he does not see the lizard that has just had intercourse with the moon.

Christina Miller

"Sun King At My Home"

My psychiatrist stands guard, his feet embedded in the desert soil and leaning slightly askew, as me and myself, masquerading as the dogs at the door, enter my house.

He did save my life all in all.

Christina Miller

"Angry Blue Madonna"

I am the Blue Madonna. I am Her. I am angry. The Earth is alive with watchfulness, its anger rising. I remove myself from intercession with mankind; I allow what is happening to continue. I am at peace. I watch you.

Christina Miller

ABOUT THE AUTHOR

Life is more than strange. There is an underlying theme to a life. We are like little books. I was born, had bad parenting, was a so-so parent myself. I always talked to God as a child and when I grew up and became deranged by self and circumstance I turned deeply and reverently towards the Great Mystery to save me. Ultimately that paid off.

I became an artist, I was always an artist, but I just didn't make any money at it. I prospered for a while on a mission to share the mysteries I had discovered at the very edge of the Universe. I was delighted and enthused to be alive, alive in a way that I had never experienced.

It wore off.

Now I am back at the beginning, the time before enlightenment. I have rolled the stone up hill and it has come crashing down again, always again. I did not know this years ago. There is no real reason to roll the stone uphill. The Mystery is as illusive on a mountain top as in a valley.

My art has continued to evolve beyond these densely strange paintings. I invite you to see how my art has transformed: www.iconfusion.com

As always, many blessings for you and all whom you love.

Christina Miller

"ALTERED LANDSCAPES"

Christina Miller

www.ingramcontent.com/pod-product-compliance
Lightning Source LLC
Chambersburg PA
CBHW050843290526
45792CB00002B/508